Litter Free

In the hope of contributing to the well-being of all.

Claude Bois

Litter Free

Guiding Your Cat's Elimination Behaviors: House-training, Uncleanness, Marking, Handling Changes, Permanent Sand Litter, Water Litter, Toilet Training

by Claude Bois

First paperback edition.

ISBN: 9781795783347

Disclaimer

This book is for informational purposes only. It is not intended to replace any treatment prescribed by a pet behaviorist or veterinarian. It is not intended to dictate what constitutes reasonable or appropriate action for dealing with pet behavior or health issues. If you have questions regarding a medical condition or behavior issue, always seek the advice of a veterinarian or a qualified pet behaviorist.

The reader assumes all risk and responsibility for the use of the information in this book. The author expressly disclaims any liability for loss, damage, or injury caused, directly or indirectly, by reliance on the information in this book. Any perceived slight to any individual, organization, product, or service is unintentional.

Table of contents

Foreword

I was lucky enough to be born on a farm in the sixties. I could spend hours observing animal and insect behaviors. As farmers, my parents had many not neutered cats. Some were having kittens in the attic, others in the barn. I played with them a lot and learned from them, following my instinct as to how to interact with them. That's how I fell in love with those very special fellows. Then my parents moved to the city, and I suddenly got access to books from a huge local library to satisfy my growing curiosity.

I read quite a few books about cats, but one stood out as written by someone who really knew about cat learning and behavior. Despite the fact that the science behind animal training dates back to the fifties, undertaking the training of a cat was still considered by most cat owners in the eighties as proof of ignorance and disrespect toward cats. Personally, I read this book with great interest, and it taught me many things, including how to train cats to eliminate in a toilet. It is unfortunate that I can't remember either the name of the author or the title of this book, since I returned it to the library so long ago.

In the nineties I studied cognitive science at McGill University. That's how I acquired my knowledge of the science behind learning and behavior in general. Then, around 2009, I found another book that revived my interest in teaching and training: *Don't Shoot the Dog!* by Karen Pryor. For me, this book was the masterpiece that bridged the gap between the science I had learned and its application in daily life.

Since 2010 I have been researching all aspects of pet care. I now plan to write a book collection aimed at giving pet owners the knowledge necessary to free themselves from the influence of special interest groups intent on selling them products and services.

One evening while I was watching cat videos on YouTube, I wound up watching some about cats being toilet trained. What I saw made me worry that cat owners would try this without the necessary information to succeed, which would inevitably produce unclean cats. I then went on Amazon and searched for books on the subject. I read their descriptions and readers' comments, then I browsed through those on Kindle Unlimited. All that got me even more worried. Knowing that uncleanliness is the main reason for cats being abandoned, I felt the urge to intervene. I therefore decided to set aside my other book projects to write this one: *Litter Free.*

One thing that bothered me is that the procedure they use still has the same flaws as the one I used back in the eighties. Sure, this procedure can work, but it is prone to all sorts of problems. Moreover, it is very demanding for the cat and very difficult and inconvenient for the owner. What I present here is an improved method.

1) I discuss everything to consider in order to reduce the risk of problems.

2) I present specific strategies to prevent inappropriate elimination.

3) I explain my unique method to ensure that the cat recognizes the toilet as "the right place to go."

4) I describe my strategy to guide the cat to place himself properly on the seat.

5) My process removes unnecessary, error-prone steps.

6) I reorder the steps so that when he moves to the real toilet, the cat knows how to pee and poo right into the bowl without making any accidents on the seat.

7) With my method, there is no gadget to remove from the seat and reinstall in order to allow people to use the toilet.

8) With my method, no litter grain will ever fall into the toilet bowl.

9) You won't need to become an expert at shaping behavior to succeed with the method I present here. And your cat won't need any special talent either, even though he probably is the most talented cat in the world to you!

Around 2003 I developed a new way to deal with litter and feces. I called it a "permanent sand litter." It was originally intended for small dogs but is perfect for cats too. I never got it patented because it was specifically designed to allow any pet owner to replicate it inexpensively.

Before I wrote this book, I reviewed the products that were available at that time. I noticed one cat litter product that shared some characteristics with my concept, and one dog potty product that presented other similarities with it. No product on the market offers all the advantages my permanent sand litter has. Maintenance costs for the permanent sand litter are extremely low.

While writing this book, I also developed another way to deal with cat feces. It is perfect for people whose bathrooms is too crowded. It can be re-created at low cost and maintenance costs are nearly zero. I call it a "water litter".

My improved method of toilet training, my permanent sand litter, and my water litter are made public in this book (paperback and e-book versions) for the first time. This is not available on web sites or on videos.[1]

While studying computer science, I learned a powerful technique to solve complex problems. The trick was to divide a big problem into smaller sections, and to repeat the process until all that remains are small problems that can be solved quickly and easily. Then, all we would need to do is take these individual solutions and connect them in order to create one big solution. In this book, you will learn many basic principles. You will learn how to use these principles in various simple scenarios. You will then learn how to combine these solutions to solve more complex problems. In the end, you will realize that you have all the building blocks required to reach your

---

[1] If you happen to see a copy of my method, my permanent sand litter, or my water litter somewhere else, please let me know at LitterFreeFreedom@yahoo.com

personal goals. Please don't try to skip any sections because you "just" want to train your cat to use a toilet. You really need to read them all, and assimilate them well, before you can understand the requirements for proper toilet training.

Finally, the ultimate purpose of this book is the same as that of the other books I intend to write. It is about empowerment: giving pet owners the knowledge to free themselves from the dictates of the industry.

Note: The text regularly uses the first person "I" as a constant reminder that the examples are what I, the author, would do in the different scenarios I present. What you will then choose to do is entirely up to you.

PART I

What Are the Videos Missing?

We humans have our own way of perceiving things. We tend to pay attention to what we see and to ignore the rest. This is partly due to our extremely well-developed visual system. Things are different for cats. Knowing the main differences between the human and feline sensory systems is a basic prerequisite of being able to change a cat's litter habits successfully. The same is true about understanding behavioral sequences in order to identify elements that may affect a cat's elimination process. On the other hand, cats and humans both have the ability to adapt to new situations, to make mental associations, and to learn what constitutes proper behavior. It is important to consider all of these elements in order to efficiently develop a method that can works for one's unique situation. Has any video showing a cat peeing or pooing in the toilet explained this? All those videos achieve is making you feel sorry that your cat isn't doing the same.

This book gives you the knowledge, and, therefore, the power, to guide your cat so he can learn to pee and poo where you choose. My guidelines will help you choose a new litter type that fits your personal objectives, whatever they are. Do you want to use less wrapping, to stop carrying heavy litter bags, to save money, to protect your floors, to reduce cleaning time, or reduce bad odors?

Sensory System

Let's now compare the senses in cats and humans.

Vision: Cats do see better than humans in dim light, yet they perceive colors with less intensity even in good light. They don't see reds. On the other hand, they see blues, greens, and yellows as well as all shades of grey from white to black. A red object would look black to a cat. The angle of net vision of a cat is 200 degrees plus thirty degrees less net on both sides. In humans, the angle of net vision is 180 degrees, plus twenty degrees less net on both sides.

Hearing: Cats can hear high frequencies and lower sound levels better than humans. They are also better than humans at locating where a sound comes from.

Touch: Cats have vibrissae to help them navigate in the dark and to sense small vibrations.

Balance: Cats have a better sense of equilibrium.

Agility: Proportionally, cats can jump much farther and much higher than humans.

Taste: This sense is less developed in cats than in humans.

Smell: Cats are about forty times more sensitive to odors than humans and can distinguish thousands of odors.

Jacobson organ ("vomero-nasal"): This organ detects pheromones (sexual hormones). It is functional in cats, but almost nonexistent in humans.

These differences are very important to consider when changing a cat's habitat. If we only consider the visual aspects of a cat's environment, we may be convinced that we made a small change when, in fact, from the cat's point of view, we changed many things.

Think of those videos that are supposed to show us how to train a cat to pee and poo in the toilet. They don't tell us that we need to pay special attention to smells, vibrations, sounds, and so forth. Every change in each of these categories makes a big difference to a cat.

Whenever possible, we should change just one aspect of the cat's habitat at a time. The more senses a modification to his environment affects, the more likely the cat will feel uncomfortable.

Elimination Process

In order to avoid creating behavioral problems, it is important to understand how elimination works and what a cat's specific needs are.

Behavioral Sequence

A behavioral sequence is a bit like a ritual. It is a sequence of actions always performed in approximately the same way. While human rituals are founded primarily on cultural distinctions, behavioral sequences in animals are essentially based on instinct and on some learning from observation and imitation. Examples of behavioral sequences are hunting, toileting, sleeping, encounters with others, reproduction, and elimination.

A cat's behavioral sequence for elimination involves:

1) Finding a location away from eating and sleeping areas.

2) Finding a location with an absorbent soil.

3) Scraping and digging a hole.

4) Adopting a squatting posture with posterior legs bent.

5) Urinating or defecating.

6) Scraping again to cover the feces:

   a) It is believed that this final scraping is triggered by the smell of feces.

   b) When a cat urinates or defecates close to the border of his territory, chances are higher that he will leave his urine or feces exposed as a sign of his presence.

   c) The farther from his sleeping and eating places a cat urinates or defecates, the higher the chances that he will leave his urine or feces exposed.

An important aspect of behavioral sequences is that an action leads to the next (i.e. increases the likelihood of the next action), until the full sequence is completed.

Another thing to understand about behavioral sequences is that, when an action can't be completed as it should, it tends to be replaced by something else. For example, if a cat hides behind a plant, folds his legs, looks thru a window, and sees a bird that he would normally jump to catch…, you'd better not move your hand anywhere close to him. He may instinctively jump to catch it. The hunting sequence has started (hiding, folding his legs, detecting a prey's movement) and it creates the urge to complete it.

In some videos, we can see cats that, having urinated or defecated in a toilet, will scrape the toilet seat even though there is no material for covering their feces. Some cats need to do this in order to complete their behavioral sequence. Eventually, some cats will "wake up" and stop on their own. I believe it is very important not to try to stop them.

In one video, the cat is moving around on the toilet seat, trying to find a position to pee. When the cat finally stops moving and starts to pee, the person who is filming advises the viewers to ‘help’ the cat by moving his leg in a specific direction. She is instructing them as to what she considers “the right position.” Then, she proceeds to move the cat’s back leg.

It is true that the cat was probably in an uncomfortable position. It is also true that the position in which she places him looks more appropriate. Additionally, she made the move very delicately. Still, I am convinced that most cats would try to find a place where they would not be disturbed rather than using the toilet.

I must insist that I would avoid any interaction (except the “pee-poo song”, as explained later) with a cat in the middle of his elimination sequence. The step-by-step procedure I present for toilet training progressively guides the cat to stay out of the litter grains and ends with the cat standing on the seat properly. If a cat makes misguided pee or poo, it would occur before the cat is moved to the real toilet. I would then just clean up after the cat is gone and expect him to do better next time.

Marking or Elimination

In order to judge whether the training is going well or not, it is important to distinguish between two different behaviors.

Typical Marking

Peeing is done in an upward posture, with a hind leg lifted.

Pee is deposited on a vertical surface.

Pee is produced in a limited amount, just enough to leave a trace of odor.

On rare occasions, marking can be made with poo. In that case cats make no attempt to hide it.

It is more common in males, but females can also do it.

It is more frequently observed in unneutered cats, but neutered cats can also do it.

Improper elimination is more likely to occur when a cat shares his habitat with other cats.

Marking can stem from or increase with stress.

Marking is a normal, instinctive behavior. Therefore, it is difficult to stop it entirely.

Preventing Marking

Although spayed females generally mark less frequently than intact males, it helps to avoid having too many cats in a small space. Keep in mind that marking is the way a cat uses his odor to tell others that he lives there, that this is his territory. When a cat uses his front paws and claws to scrape, he leaves his odor (there are odor-secreting glands in the paws). Consequently, not declawing cats and giving them scraping surfaces helps to reduce marking. Cats also leave their odor by rubbing their face (odor-secreting glands there too) and flanks on all surfaces. A good cleaning to these surfaces will only increase the likelihood that a cat resumes marking, possibly with urine.

Typical Elimination

Typical elimination is done in a squatting posture, for both pee and poo.

Pee or poo is deposited on a horizontal surface and/or in a hole.

A significant amount of urine is evacuated when emptying the bladder.

An attempt is made to cover it.

Preventing Inappropriate Elimination

Cat behavior specialists are mainly consulted for inappropriate elimination behavior. They will check:

1) If the cat is sick or has recently been sick. For example, if the cat has/had pain while eliminating in a litter, he may associate going in the litter with experiencing pain. This leads to litter avoidance. Note that cats are well known to suffer in silence; they may hide it when they are sick (ex: urinary disease, diabetes,

kidney disease, etc.), so owners are not aware of their problems.

2) If the cat has somehow developed an aversion for his usual litter substrate, or if his usual substrate has been replaced by one that he is not used to or one that he dislikes.

3) If the location of the litter has changed.

4) If a closed litter was changed for an open litter, or vice-versa.

5) If the litter is large enough and kept clean.

6) If something bothers the cat on his way to or while he is in his litter. For example, other cats or children, sudden noise, vibration.

7) If the cat is stressed for any reason. Cats can experience stress due to various conflictual situations with other cats, dogs, humans. Cats can also be stressed due to disruptions in the house (children fighting, divorce, renovations, etc.).

8) If the litter really is located in the best place for the cat.

As you can see, any change in the elimination routine should not be taken lightly. Carefully evaluate any changes to the location of the litter, in the substrate, of the smells, of the sounds, of the vibrations, or of the décor and implement them with all possible precautions.

Too many changes at once, unsuitable changes, or too rapid a succession of changes, will stress the cat out and will initiate or increase inappropriate behavior.

It is extremely important to find the cause and correct the situation promptly when a cat starts inappropriate elimination or marking before a bad habit gets established.

Adjusting for More Than One Cat

I find it better to have one elimination place for each cat, but there are cases when many cats accept going in the same place. This is more likely to happen with sibling (or raised together since young age) and spayed cats.

However, the main concern is the cleanliness of the spot in terms of material residue and in terms of smell. Cleanliness is easily achieved when cats are using a toilet.

Some people recommend having one more litter than the number of cats, as a safeguard, in case the litter is not cleaned as often as it is recommended.

Learning

To teach new behavior to a cat we need a basic understanding of how he learns. More specifically, to get a cat to learn to go in a new place for elimination, we can use:

His ability to get used to new situations.

His ability to make new mental associations.

His ability to shape his behavior to reach his goals.

Getting Used to New Situations

All of us who have had cats know that they can easily get startled or afraid of things that are new to them. Some examples are:

New sounds.

New odors.

New places.

New textures.

Something that starts to move when it usually doesn’t.

Something that starts to make a sound when it usually doesn’t.

Unusual vibrations

On the other hand, cats can also get used to those things simply through repetitive exposure to them and/or exposure to them for a long period of time. This process is called habituation.

What can go wrong? It is very important that the new stimulus be moderate. Otherwise, the cat can get an opposite reaction called sensitization; the cat starts to fear the situation as well as any situation which, from his point of view, resembles the situation when/where he was terrified.

Making New Mental Associations

Learn What to Expect

I hope you have experienced what I did in my childhood. Coming home and smelling one of your favorite meals cooking; just the smell of it can make someone start feeling hungry.

You may have learned that when your mother calls you 'honey' you can expect her to be kind to you, leading you to feel relaxed. You may have learned that when she calls you by your full name you can expect her to be upset, leading you to feel stressed.

Cats can learn cues from their surroundings that make them expect things to come. Those cues can make them hungry, relaxed, stressed, trigger the need to pee, and so on.

Pee-poo Song

This step is optional but often useful and easy to implement. It can help to overcome problems, so it is worth the effort.

I chose a melody that I liked. Now, I simply repeat "pee-poo pee-poo pee-poo" over and over using that melody each time I happen to see my cat pee or poo. I must sing it in the same way in every instance. So, I recorded myself to help me remember the exact tune. The volume needs to be loud enough for the cat to hear me well, but not so loud as to disturb him or stop him. I must use this song <u>only:</u>

1) Just before my cat starts to eliminate.
2) While my cat is eliminating and stop singing when he is done.

I keep doing this for the cat's whole life. When that conditioning is well-established, I can start to use the song when I want to make the cat eliminate. My cat will "feel like peeing or pooing" whenever he hears me sing that song. If he is withholding his pee or poo, it will start his elimination sequence. That can be extremely helpful when making litter changes and when traveling.

I would wait after at least fifty pairings of the song with an elimination before I try to start the cat's elimination with it.

I must use it only when I have a good reason to believe that the cat is withholding his pee or poo. It is important because each time I sing it, if the cat doesn't end up eliminating, it progressively erases this conditioning.

Learn What to Do

Behaviorists know well that cats' behavior is easily shaped. Many cat owners once thought that cats were difficult to train because they were applying the same techniques as they would with dogs. The first rule in training an animal is to know what motivates him. A dog's main motivation is to please its owner. The cat's main motivation is its personal comfort. All cats can learn very sophisticated patterns of behavior if we make sure this contributes to their satisfaction and/or comfort.

On some toilet training videos, we can see and hear people praising the cats while they are on the toilet and giving them treats as they finish.

Also, a couple of well-intentioned cat owners have written a book where they describe how they toilet trained their cat. They used a technique like what I learned in the eighties, but they also used praise and food treats each time the cat finished peeing or pooing on the toilet. They honestly warned the readers that training their cat took them a long time and to stay home and watch! Then they mentioned that the cat waits for them to be home and watching before he relieves himself! Personally, this is the last thing in the world I would want.

While the cat is peeing or pooing, I do not interfere in any way. If I happen to be there, I look away so that the cat doesn't get distracted. As explained above, the cat is in the middle of a behavioral sequence; interfering is like waking up a sleepwalker. The only thing I do <u>if I happen to be there</u> is to sing the pee-poo song.

While a cat holds his pee or poo, he feels a growing discomfort. When the cat releases his pee or poo, he feels relieved. Therefore, peeing and pooing are self-gratifying actions. Biologists call it a return to homeostasis, meaning a feeling of balance, of well-being. As seen above, its own wellbeing is the cat's main motivation, so it is not necessary to give him a treat after he pees or poos. It is important to understand that the cat shapes his behavior himself in order to adapt to a changing environment.

Meaning of "treats"

Whenever I write "I give the cat a treat," it is in the broad sense of the word "treat." What I mean is to do something that will induce a positive response from the cat. It is possible that some cats will be thrilled by a specific kind of food. In that case, the "treat" can be just that. Other cats will be thrilled by a game, or possibly an object they like to chase and catch. Others will love that you talk to them, or that you pet them. Let these be their "treats."

Also, all cats need to eat, and if given the choice, they will eat about sixteen times per twenty-four hours. Eating and drinking, like peeing or pooing, are self-gratifying actions. In some cases, I can get a cat to like a room simply by leaving his food and water there. The catch is that later, to turn that place into an elimination place, I must remove the food and water and clean the place, so there is no food odor left. If I have a very independent cat, or if I am out of time, I still have this option as a last resort.

The method I present here does not need the owners to do any "behavior shaping" in the technical sense. I know from scientific knowledge and first-hand experience that it is neither needed nor helpful. I only use "treats" to facilitate habituation by creating and positive association[2].

---

[2] Experts would call this "classical conditioning"

Behavioral Sequence vs Learning

Scientists need to isolate each aspect of behavior they want to study in a well-controlled environment. Wisely designed laboratory settings allow them to find the rules that underlie those behaviors. Ethologists and behaviorists have distinguished behavioral sequencing from learning. Then, scientists have categorized learning in distinct parts: habituation (getting used to new surroundings or events), classical conditioning (learning what to expect by association), and operant conditioning (learning what to do to achieve one's goal). In real life situations many or all of those aspects of behavior and learning are often active in one single event.

At some point in the past, scientists believed that fixed patterns like elimination were completely unchangeable. Today, it is clear that the ability to get used to novelty and to adapt to change is strong enough to allow many cats to learn seemingly unusual behaviors like peeing and pooing in a toilet. That ability stays intact for the cats' lives. Yet, we need to respect limits and follow specific rules as presented below.

PART II

Avoiding Problems

Here is a list of key steps for avoiding problems while changing litter habits.

Smell

Instinctively, when a cat wants to pee or poo, he keeps away from places that smell like vinegar (acetic acid). Additionally, when a cat wants to pee or poo, his instinct is to look for places that smell like chlorine (sodium hypochlorite). I try to use just those two smells, always very diluted, to guide the cat where I want him to go. I avoid everything that has perfumes; whether it be litter grains or the soap used to clean the litter and the surrounding areas. To trap odors, I only use baking soda (sodium bicarbonate). Doing so reduces the risk of having a cat who avoids his litter due to a smell he dislikes.

Cleaning

I use a chlorine solution (sodium hypochlorite) for cleaning litters. It is the product used to bleach laundry and to clean toilet's rooms and bowls. I take a product that don't have added perfume. The concentration of chlorine in products vary for brand to brand so it affects the quantity I use. I follow the instruction recommended for general bathroom cleaning when I must clean a litter box or water litter. When I need to disinfect the permanent sand, I use the instruction recommended for toilet's bowls cleaning, with hot water, and let stand 20 minutes. In all cases, it is important to rinse very well. Even thought cats are attracted to go pee or poo in area that smell chlorine, it must be a very faint residual smell that we can barely perceive.

When a litter is moved, I wash the floor where the litter was. I use my regular product and add one teaspoon (five milliliters) of white vinegar (5 percent acetic acid) in one gallon (four liters) of water.

If the litter was on carpet:

1) I spread three teaspoons (fifteen milliliters) of baking soda (sodium bicarbonate) over the carpet and help it penetrate by rubbing my hand against it.

2) I wait twenty minutes.

3) I vacuum the carpet.

4) I lightly spray a solution of one part white vinegar to four parts water.

Stability

Whatever setup is intended for the cat's use, it must always be stable. Each intermediary setup needs to be stable too. If the cat jumps on an unstable litter once, he may decide to avoid it from them on.

Even though cats are athletes and often jump on unstable things, when they want to eliminate they are in a special state of mind. They instinctually know that they are vulnerable when peeing or pooing, so they look for a well-known quiet and stable place. It takes specific training to alter that natural tendency.

Sensory Changes

Limit the number of sensory changes: Each change should affect the smallest number of senses. Example: A change that affects the way the litter looks but not how it feels (texture) or how it smells is much easier to accept than a change that affects those three senses together. Reviewing "Cat Sensory System" to see the main differences with humans will help avoid that kind of error.

Dimensional Changes

Stay with small, progressive dimensional change: like quantity, shape, size, and others. Example: To change the amount of sand in a litter from six inches to half an inch (15 cm to 1.5 cm) deep is better done in many small steps. Say six steps, each lasting seven days seems reasonable.

Combined Changes

Avoid combining types of changes. Try to avoid making both sensory and dimensional changes all at once. Example: Changing a litter from rough grains, pine smelling litter to one that contains fine grains with the smell of lavender counts for two changes. I try to make only one change at a time. Here, I can't separate the new litter grain size from the smell. So, I must progressively mix more of the new litter into the old one. To adjust, I would add the new litter twice as slowly than if it was only a change in smell or in the size of the litter grain.

Solving Problems

What else could I do to find and correct a problem?

Since cats have sensitivities out of the range of human perception, it is always possible that the cat gets disturbed by some smell, some noise, or some vibration that I just can't detect. To get around this, I may:

1) Switch to another brand of litter: This should work if the cat has developed an aversion to his current litter. This is a rare situation where it would help to change to something different.

2) Buy a new litter box: This should work if the cat has developed an aversion to his current litter box. This is also a rare situation where it would help to change to something different.

3) Wash the room, the litter (or the bowl or the toilet), and fill it with brand new grains (or water). If using litter, keep the same brand and variety. This should

work if a disturbing odor is there (ex: another animal has left his odor in the room or in the litter).

4) Move the litter to another room. This should work if the cat is disturbed by something in the current room. This can also work if the cat is disturbed on his way to the current room (ex: a cat or a dog that bothers him).

Respect

Or, when to slow down, stop, step back, or even give up?

This chapter is the most important one in this book. If you misunderstood the rest of this book, but get this chapter right, it should keep you and your cat out of real trouble.

The most frequent cause of cat abandonment is uncleanliness. Cats that do their pees and/or poos in inappropriate places. I chose to write this book precisely because, having seen videos on "cats toilet training," I became afraid that this problem of uncleanliness would become even more frequent due to the temptation to try it out while lacking vital information.

Changing a cat's litter habits is a delicate process; that, I am sure you have understood by now. Understanding a theory and having the wisdom to admit that we don't know everything are two different things. Even assuming you did understand everything in this book and are smart enough to adapt it to your own specific situation, many things could still go wrong. On my side, I am far from perfect, so this book can't be either.

Before going ahead, for the love of your cat, please swear to yourself that you will slow down, stop, step back or even give up should your desire to make a change in litter habit become a risk to your cat's hygiene and health.

To help in making wise decisions throughout the process of changing litter habits, I've created these guidelines:

1) When a cat is not clean, when he does occasionally eliminate (not just mark) in inappropriate places, it is never wise to demand that he adapt to changes. First, I would solve the current elimination problem. Then, when the cat is perfectly clean, I would wait for at least a month before changing anything.

2) In the event of a clear marking behavior that has been going on before the change in litter habit was

initiated, that has not intensified since the start of the changes, I would go on with the change in litter habit.

3) In the event of a clear marking behavior that has started or intensified after the change in litter habit was initiated, I would go back one step in the change. Either the cat is stressed due to an error I am making, or I am mistakenly interpreting an elimination as a marking. Both mean that I need to find the problem and solve it before going on.

4) In the event of a clear elimination behavior out of the selected place, I would assume I made an error in the way I am making changes. I need to go back one step and wait one week. During that time, I need to find the probable cause of the error and resume progress only after I figure out a way to resolve it.

After five pees or poos in total out of the litter, that qualifies as inappropriate elimination, I would feel that I must give up. Here, 'I must give up' means I must go one (or more) steps back from the setting that caused the uncleanliness and stop there; no more changes.

If that change in litter habit is very important for me, I would try to figure out if there are other solutions that would achieve the same goal. Of course, it is best to find a solution that does not involve a change in litter habit. If those other solutions all need changes in litter habit, I would wait after at least four months of cleanliness (not including marking which is acceptable) before starting any other process.

PART III

What Is My Real Goal?

Before I decide on what I want as a new litter habit for my cat, I should evaluate what my real goals are and my order of priority. It is important to do it well and before I start making any changes. I don't want to invest time and energy heading in the wrong direction. More importantly, I don't want my cat to become confused due to many unnecessary changes.

Here is a list of what I can think of; complete it with your own goals.

- A more environmentally-friendly product (less packaging, compostable grains, no need to transfer pee and poo in small plastic bags).
- Stop carrying heavy litter bags.
- Fewer bad odors in the house (a litter that better absorbs odor and/or pee and poo that can be flushed

in a toilet instead of staying in the garbage can where they continue to emit odors).

- Shorter cleaning times.
- Saving money.
- Protecting my wood floor from hard litter grains.
- No more dust, or at least less dust.
- My cat needs to have cleaner paws; he often jumps on the table and counter.
- I want something that won't harm a kitten or cats when swallowed.

What Are My Limitations?

It is great to want the perfect litter, but I also must take my limitations into account. Here are a few examples:

- I don't have much time to invest in the transition. I need a change of litter type that is easy to make.

- I have only one toilet and there are ten people using it. The door is often closed. I'd better not move the cat there.

- My cat is old, overweight, or has joint pain. He needs an easy to reach installation, and one that doesn't require him to adopt a difficult posture.

Choosing My Cat's New Litter Setting

To make the final choice for my cat's future litter setting, I need an overview of some of the possibilities. I also need to know the advantages and disadvantages of each option. Finally, to make an informed choice, I need a list of all the necessary steps.

This is exactly what the next chapters present. The examples are there to give you tricks and tips that you can later use and combine to achieve your specific goals. It is useful to read them no matter what you end up doing.

Leafy Green Pellet Litter

Picture 1: This is what pellets look like.

What It Is

Alfalfa pellets are small, compressed cylinders of a dry leafy herb often served as rabbits' food. The variety for growing, pregnant, or nursing rabbits usually has a high percentage of alfalfa. Pellets that have a high percentage of Timothy grass are also great. It is the leafy green ingredients which brings the odor-absorbing property. I do not use the variety intended for snakes' litter because it is treated with chemical products for preventing fungus. I would not use the natural dry herb (not compressed in pellets) because it is too light and would spill around the house.

Characteristics

-Ideal for cats and kitten who tend to eat litter grains. Also, great if the dog eats cat's poos.

-Low dust. Good quality "fresh" product has a low amount of dust. The dust is not toxic.

-Low odor. Alfalfa and Timothy grass are leafy plant full of chlorophyll, and chlorophyll is an effective natural odor absorbing agent. The alfalfa or Timothy pellets for rabbits are often mix with other eatable plant products that may have less chlorophyll. The greener the pellets, the more chlorophyll there is.

-Safe for wood floor. Sand and some litter grains can scratch wood floor finish, eatable pellets are less likely to do so.

-Compostable: Being an herb, it's compostable. I would not put it in my food garden compost bac because my bac is too small to reach the high temperature that kill bacterizes. My city has a big composting system that destroy bacterizes so it would be fine there.

-Flushable. My toilet is linked to the city sewer, so I feel comfortable flushing small amount of alfalfa pellets. When I buy a new product, I put a spoonful of it in a cup of water and wait five minutes. If it turns into a purée, then I consider it safe to flush.

-Less heavy to carry: For the same volume, standard litter (zeolite: porous grainy rocks) is heavier, and sand is much heavier.

-The cost depends on where I buy it. If I buy it in small quantities in a pet shop, it can cost as much as top-quality clumping litter. If I buy it from a farmer's co-op, it can be very cheap. I wouldn't mind buying food pellets for cows if they are the same size as those for rabbits and made with leafy green plants. Using wood or paper-based pellets instead would not be the same: these are not odor-repellent (I would need to use baking soda), it would not be edible, and I would not feel comfortable flushing it in my toilet. If the product is intended for combustion, I would need to check that it does not have a starter agent.

Cleaning Pellet Litter

I scoop out poos as I would with granular litter; with a slotted scoop or spatula. If the pellets I use are flushable (see the test described above), I put it directly in the toilet and flush. I can also use some toilet paper instead of a scoop if the poo is not buried too deep.

When the cat pees on pellets, most of it flows to the bottom of the litter. There, it takes about twenty minutes for it to be absorbed by the pellets. Those pellets, filled with urine, will clump in the bottom of the litter and stick there. I then need to slowly transfer the dry contents into a bucket. To do so, I gently tilt the litter until the dry contents roll into the bucket. I then use a spatula to dump the left-over clump of pellets sticking to the bottom of the litter box. Even though I use flushable pellets, I don't put more than a cup (250 ml) of clumped pellets in the toilet before flushing.

- I rinse the litter, clean it, and dry the litter box.

- Alternatively, I could use a plastic bag in the litter box to be dumped in a garbage can, but I would then lose many of the advantages that leafy green pellets provide.

I check that the pellets in the bucket don't smell bad. I also check that there is no trace of fungus (black or white moss) on them. If the cat has not been sick and everything looks normal, I can transfer the pellets back to the litter box and add new pellets up to three or four inches thick (7.5 to 10 centimeters)

Permanent Sand Litter

Picture 2: On the left, the top box with holes. I made just a few holes, but it is best to make one every ¾ inch (19 millimeters). The dark line shows where to put the glue.

Picture 3: On the left, top box with a glued geotextile.

Picture 4: Handles to help separate the top box from the bottom one.

What It Is

I use two identical litter boxes stacked inside one another. On the bottom of the top box, I drill holes, one 1/8-inch (3 millimeters) diameter hole every ¾ inch (19 millimeters). I apply a line of glue inside the top box, along the circumference of its bottom, and place a geotextile to cover the holes and the glue. I stick the geotextile in place and let the glue dry. I add three to four inches (7.5 to 10 centimeters) of sand to the top box (over the geotextile). I now have sand over a type of sieve over a sealed container (the lower box).

To make it easier to manipulate and clean, I install a handle on one side of each box. To do so, I drill two holes and join them with a cord, adding a node at each end to fix it.

I choose the litter boxes so that:

1) When stacked, they leave an empty space of about half an inch to one inch (one to two and a half

centimeters) between the bottom of the top box and the bottom of the lower box.

2) When stacked, both boxes are stable.

3) Both boxes have all sides at least six inches (15 centimeters) high.

I can use sand for a sandbox or sand for a pool filter. The last is less dusty but is more expensive.

Characteristics

-Safe for cats and kittens who tend to eat litter grains; not so good to eat, but at least it's not toxic and not clumping in the gut.

-No dust. After a few rinses, all dust will have drained off.

-Low odor. The urine will drain to the bottom, in the sealed part, and the rest will be rinsed out every day. I can also place a sodium bicarbonate tissue bag close by for more odor protection.

-Compostable: I always reuse the same sand so there is nothing to compost except the poo. I would not put poos in my food garden compost bag because my bag is too small to reach the high temperature that kills bacteria. My city has a big composting system that destroys bacteria so it would be perfect there.

-Flushable: My toilet is connected to the city sewer, and flushing produces a good flow of water. It's strong enough to carry away a few bits of sand. Note that I first shake off the excess sand in the litter box. I can make no guarantee as to what would work with other people's toilets.

-Heavy to carry, but only once: For the same volume, sand is heavier than standard litter (zeolite: porous grainy rocks) and much heavier than pellets.

-Very low-cost: I need to invest in two litter boxes, some glue, a geotextile and two cords. Then, I only need to buy the amount of sand that will fill one litter box. Afterward, I need to buy a few more cups of sand once a year. I also must pay for hot water and chlorine cleaner.

The total is much cheaper than the least expensive standard litter (ex: zeolite) which constantly needs replacement.

-Not safe for wood floors: Sand can scratch wood floor finishes.

- One plastic bag a year and zero space used in my garbage.

Cleaning Permanent Sand Litter

Once a day:

1) I scoop out poos, as in a granular litter, with a slotted scoop. I shake off the excess sand and I put the poos directly in my toilet and flush.

2) I rinse the sand with cold water, then wait five minutes for it to drain.

3) I remove the lower box and flush its contents (water and urine). I rinse it and put it back in place.

Once a month:

1) I scoop out poos.

2) I give the cat an opportunity to pee or poo before I start this cleaning; scraping the litter should get him to do so if he needs to.

3) In the bathroom, I close the door to make sure the cat can't come in.

4) I rinse the sand with cold water, then wait five minutes for it to drain.

5) I remove the lower box and flush its contents (water and urine), then I put it back in place.

6) I place the doubled litter in a bathtub or in a shower that can withstand chlorine solution.

7) In a bucket, I prepare a mix of hot water and chlorine.

8) I pour the hot water-chlorine mix over the sand until it is all covered.

9) I let it stand twenty minutes.

10) Wearing gloves, I remove the sand box and put it down on the base of the bath or shower. I flush the water-chlorine from the lower box.

11) I let it drain for five minutes, then rinse the sand box and the lower box thoroughly.

12) I let it drain another five minutes, then stack the boxes up.

13) I place the litter back where it used to be.

Is this too complicated? Then read on to the next section.

Into a Bath or Shower

Picture 5: The dark circle shows where to cut the hole in the bottom box. This is right above the bath drain and close to the side of the box.

Picture 6: For the litter to be stable in my shower, I need to place its center over the drain. The dark circle shows where to cut the hole. It is right above the shower drain.

For me, the best place to leave a permanent sand litter is by far in a bath or a shower not used regularly. It lets less sand escape to my floor. But, most importantly, it can make cleaning much easier. Of course, this is something I would only do if my bath or shower is "sand proof" because some sand will escape from the litter when the cat gets out of it[3]. Here is how I achieve it:

1) I place the lower box over the drain of the bath or shower in such a way that the drain is covered and the litter is stable.

2) In the lower box, I then mark the location of the center of the drain and drill a hole. The size of the hole should be such that a rubber stopper can block it up when I need to do the once a month cleaning.

3) I stack up the boxes and leave them in the bath or shower with the hole open over the drain.

Now, I can do the once a day cleaning very easily: I do not need to remove the sand box from the lower box. I just need to remove the poo and rinse the sand with cold

---

[3] For instance, acrylic bath and shower are easily scratched by sand.

water. The water will drain from the sand to the lower box, and from there directly into the drain. Wow!

The once a month cleaning is also much easier: I do not need to remove the sand box from the lower box either. I push the stopper in the hole from the exterior of the lower box. I do the treatment with the chlorine as above. Then I place the hole over the drain and remove the cap. I rinse thoroughly. Done!

When I need to use the bath/shower, I give the cat a chance to pee or poo (by scraping the sand and letting him do his business). If some sand has escape, I put it back in the litter. Then, I push the stopper in the hole from the exterior of the lower box and place the litter outside the bath. Then, I close the door, leaving the cat out of the bathroom, until I can place the litter back in the bath and remove the stopper.

Water Litter

I wrote previously that to pee and poo in a toilet seems like awkward behavior for a cat. But, is it really so awkward? Many animals would dig a hole, pee or poo in it, and bury it. The tendencies to do it are hard-wired as part of the cat's evolution. Those cats who did that tended to have a better survival rate. Doing so hides one's odor, thereby offering some effective protection from predators. It also reduces the contact with potential harmful bacteria and parasites. These facts apply to humans too. Now, look around the world; the use of toilets has spread widely. Whenever people can have it, they want it, and whenever they lose it, they miss it a lot! So, I suspect that there is something instinctively appealing in the use of toilets.

The cat's behavioral sequence for elimination is grounded on the very same instinctive motivations as humans. So, it just makes sense to assume that toilets have some appeal to them as well. Here, I am not implying this appeal would suffice to make cats spontaneously move from granular litter to toilets. What I am suggesting is that, once they learn to go on a toilet, their instinct will make them end up finding it great. In a toilet, pee and poo are sort of instantly buried. The odor disappears. When a cat does his pee or poo from a toilet seat, his feet won't get dirty. From a cat's point of view, that's highly valued in litter characteristics.

When we look at cats learning, with difficulty, how to place themselves to pee or poo on a toilet seat, we may think that this training is inappropriate, or even a form of torture. As for me, now that I have analyzed it, I see it as an improvement of their quality of life. But, before the actual toilet training, we need to know how to train a cat to use water litter.

What It Is

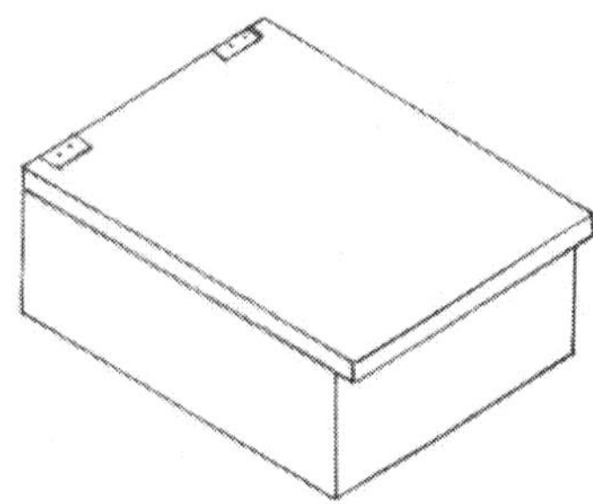

Picture 7: This is a box I could use for water litter.

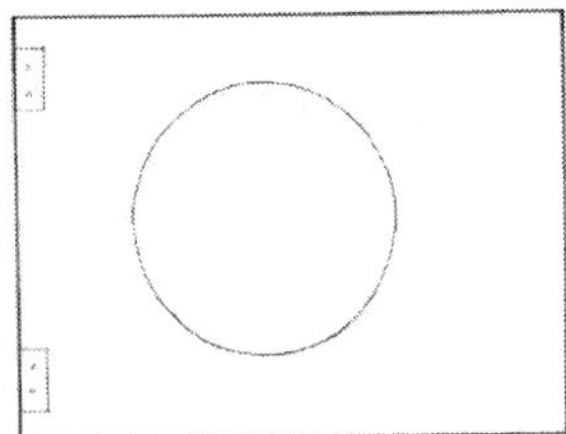

Picture 8: The circle shows where I would cut the hole on the cover of the water litter.

Water litter is a round bowl of water, about ten inches (25 centimeters) in diameter X five inches deep (13 centimeters) inside a box. The box is about fourteen x eighteen X six inches (35 X 45 X 15 centimeters). The box has a cover that can be open and closed easily with two hinges. The cover has a round hole about nine inches (23 centimeters) in diameter, over the bowl of water. The box, bowl, and cover are in an easy to clean, water-resistant material. The assembly is solid, stable, and will not tilt when the cat jumps on it. As you can guess, the cover can be a flat panel, like in the drawing above, or a toilet seat, like in the pictures below.

Picture 9a: Water litter with a toilet seat as cover.

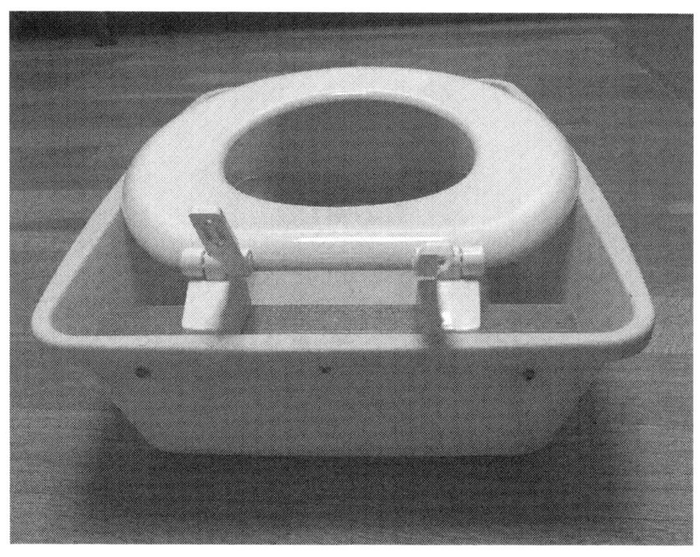

Picture 9b: Water litter back.

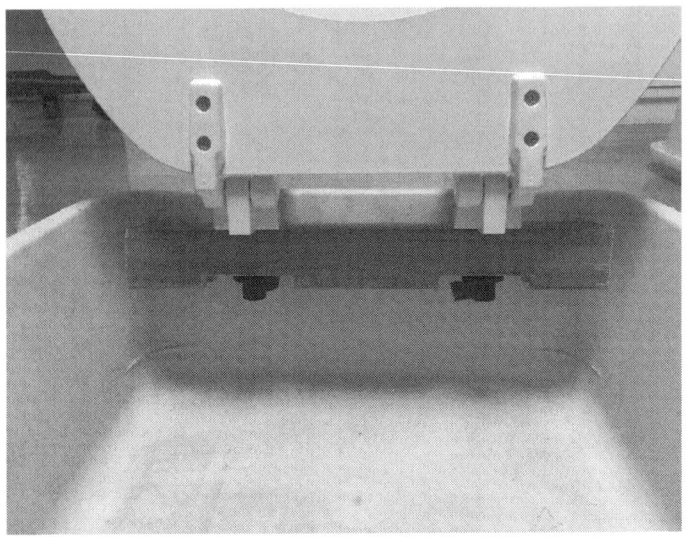

Picture 9c: Water litter inside.

Characteristics

-Ideal for cats and kittens over eight weeks of age: Kittens need to be solid enough on their feet not to fall in the water, or else they may develop an aversion. Another good point for kittens is that there is no litter grain to eat.

-Ideal for a house with many people and few toilets.

-No dust.

-Low odor: When the pee and poo fall in the water, the odors in the air are instantly greatly reduced. It is also possible to spread some baking soda (sodium bicarbonate) in the box around the bowl.

-Compostable: I would not put it in my food garden compost bag because my bag is too small to reach the high temperature that kills bacteria. My city has a big composting system that destroys bacteria so it would be perfect there.

-Flushable in any toilet!

-Easy to carry: I only need to put three inches (7.5 centimeters) of water in a bowl and bring it to the room where the litter is.

-Cost is very low. I need to buy a set of three bowls, a box, a cover and two hinges once. For upkeep, I only need water and chlorine.

-Safe for hard floors.

-If I install the water litter in a room with a carpet that is difficult to clean, I must avoid dropping dirty water on the carpet when I bring the bowl to the toilet. Because this cleaning is needed every day, over time accidents are likely to happen.

-Zero plastic bag and zero space used in your garbage.

Cleaning Water Litter

Once a day: I flush the water and rinse the bowl out thoroughly.

Once a week: I use a chlorine solution to clean the bowl, the box, and the cover.

Toilet Training

My method of toilet training uses no odd gadgets. Litter grains can never fall in the toilet bowl. I never have to install and remove anything from my toilet seat to be able to use it myself. When the cat starts to go on my toilet seat, he has already learned how to place his feet so neither urine nor poo will end up on my toilet seat.

What It Is

The cat will pee and poo at the same place as us humans do, from a toilet seat into a toilet bowl.

Characteristics

-Ideal for cats and kittens over six months of age. Kittens need to be big enough to jump out of the toilet bowl if they were to fall in there.

-Ideal for a house with many cats: The odor is so low that most cats won't mind sharing a toilet. If not, the technique “leaky toilet” described below, which leaves no odor, might be used.

-Ideal for small apartments: No extra space needed.

-No dust.

-Low odor: When the pee and poo fall in the water, the odors in the air are instantly reduced. It is also possible to spread some baking soda (sodium bicarbonate) between the back of the seat and the water tank or to use the “leaky toilet” method described below.

-Noting to put in compost.

-Directly flushable.

-Nothing to carry.

-Cost is very low: For training, I need a set of three bowls, an extra toilet seat, some cardboard, and lots of strong tape. Maintenance costs noting (except if I pay for water consumption).

-Zero plastic bags and zero space used in my garbage.

PART IV

When to Change

Changes in litter habits cause at least some stress to the cat and to its owner. Initiate changes when the cat is relaxed and confident. A cat is confident when he walks head and tail up and doesn't run away at all events when surprised.

I do not start changes in litter habits if:

1) The cat is new to the house. I wait at least two weeks after adoption or until the cat shows confident behavior.

2) The cat is sick. I wait two weeks after he gets well.

3) A new person or pet has joined, will join, or has left or is leaving the family. I wait two weeks or more if the cat doesn't get along well with the newcomer.

4) A move or renovation is expected. I wait two weeks after things have calmed down.

5) The cat is about to have kittens. I wait until the kittens are independent.

6) I am overworked: the process of change needs some extra time and effort from me, too. If an unexpected stressful event happens during the process of changing litter habits, I do not proceed to any new steps. I wait two weeks after the situation has resolved before proceeding to further steps.

Preliminary Habituation

Whenever possible, I train the cat to enjoy being in a room, and know what to expect, before I move his litter there. This familiarization phase is call habituation. Proceeding in that manner, I make sure no bad surprises could occur when the cat starts to use his litter in the room. This prevent unfortunate bad association to develop. Imagine you eat something new, and right then, you develop a new health problem. Your first reaction is to suspect the new food. Cats react like that to. For example, if a frightening noise is produced the first time the cat uses his litter in a new room, he may assume that the noise is produced by the fact that he just jumped in the litter. Hence, he may decide to stop using it.

Example of habituation: The litter is currently in the living room and my goal is to toilet train the cat.

I make sure there will never be an event that is too strong or frightening in the bathroom. If I do let that happen, I would create sensitization (= permanent fear and avoidance) instead of habituation (= confidence). I have never gotten used to the "end of cycle" buzz coming from my washing machine and dryer, so I don't expect a cat to ever be okay with it: I disabled those permanently before I let the cat in the room.

Then, I thought about the cat's sensory system. Knowing that it is different from mine, I tried to figure everything out that could possibly bother him. Those may include things that I couldn't possibly perceive.

Vibrations from a washing machine or dryer take time to progressively used to, so does flushing the toilet. Even starting the ventilation fan frightened a kitten when he first heard it. Opening a window will bring in new odors, sounds and vibrations (ex: winds, curtains that start to move, sounds from the street, etc.).

For those things that I can identify, I turn them on and give a treat to the cat if he stays or when he comes back. I repeat this method of positive association until the cat stops reacting.

For those things that I can't identify, I need to let the cat spend time in the room so that everything there will have happened many times. The easiest way is to install the cat bed and food and water bowl in the bathroom. On the other hand, I place them as far away from the toilet bowl as I can, but still in the bathroom. Note: If the bathroom is less than six feet long (two meters), I would install the cat's bed, food and water on a higher level (on a shelf or on a counter) so that it feels as separated as possible from his elimination place. The simple fact of having his food, water and a comfortable bed in the room is reinforcing. If I spend time petting and playing with him in that room, it's even better.

During the habituation period, I leave the door open.

Regularity Check

Most cats poo twice every twenty-four hours and pee more often than they poo. I would check the frequency of my cat's poo and pee before starting changes. Then, when I make changes to litter habits, if my cat used to poo twice every twenty-four hours, when sixteen hours have passed without any pee nor poo, I know there is a problem. I would then try to start the cat's elimination behavior.

If the cat is using granulated litter, it may work to scrape and dig in it like the cat would do to get the cat to come around. I would then step back and leave him to go. If no granulated litter is used and the cat is supposed to jump on the toilet seat and pee in the toilet bowl, I would place the cat on the seat and slowly step back. If necessary, in both scenarios, I would repeat this step up to nine times.

If my cat has been conditioned with a "pee-poo song," it is the perfect time to use it. I start singing while scraping or while placing the cat on the toilet seat, and I do not stop until the cat has done his business or until two minutes have passed.

If that still doesn't work, I must go back one step in my litter change procedure and figure out what I did wrong.

Confinement

I very much dislike to confine a cat but I am convinced the confinement procedure is better for both of us in some cases.

1) The cat must like the room before he is confined, so I first carry out the preliminary habituation.

2) The only absorbent horizontal surface in the room should be the cat's bed. If I have no choice but to leave other absorbent horizontal surfaces in that room, I need to cover them with plastic and affix the plastic properly so that the cat can't remove it.

    a) If the cat already has a bed, I place it in the room.

    b) If the cat doesn't have a bed, I give him one. I place the cat on its new bed and pet him there so that he stays there at least five minutes. I don't leave the room until the cat has adopted his new bed (has slept in it at least five minutes).

c) I also make sure the cat has a vertical surface to scratch and some toys.

3) I carry out the regularity check procedure.

4) I look thoroughly and often in order to find out quickly if the cat is peeing and pooing in the proper place or outside of it. I leave the cat confined until he has done a minimum of two poos and four pees at the correct place, with no inappropriate elimination. In case of an inappropriate elimination, I must go back one step in my litter change procedure and figure out what I did wrong.

5) When I release the cat, I move his bed, food, water, and toys out of the confinement room.

Anchoring

When making a change, after the cat has made twelve poos in the new setting, with no inappropriate elimination (marking doesn't count), I can go on to the next change. That generally means about six or seven days. This period is what I refer to as anchoring.

During anchoring, it is important that I keep the litter very clean to ensure that the cat doesn't start to avoid it for a reason (dirtiness) that has nothing to do with the changes I am making. Also, the cat is still looking for "the best" place to eliminate, and cleanliness is a quality he highly values.

For all anchoring period, I make sure the cat always has easy access to the room where is litter is. A cat can withhold his pee/poo for a long time. Yet, during this first anchoring stage he would start looking for another place to eliminate early in the process.

Please note that during the month after the anchoring, I make sure the cat can't find anything more like its earlier litter than the new setting, otherwise he will certainly go there.

Part V

House-training

When a cat has kittens, we call her a queen. The queen licks the young kittens' abdomens to make them eliminate. Doing so, she ingests their pees and poos. The queen keeps doing this until kittens are about one month of age and stop sucking. Later, the queen will show the kittens where to eliminate and they will imitate her. By six weeks of age, the kittens know where to go and what to do.

A kitten should not be separated from his mother and siblings before eight weeks of age at minimum. Some advocate that it should not be before twelve weeks of age. This is needed for important psychological reasons, but outside the realm of this book. So, when a kitten gets adopted and move to a new house, he is already house-trained! A newly adopted kitten's house-training is about moving a litter from one home to another at the same time than habituating a kitten to a new house.

First, let me point out that a kitten:

- Needs to pee and poo more often then an adult cat.

- Is not able to withhold his pee or poo as long as an adult cat.

- Is more than ever looking out for someone to imitate. It may suffice to scrape and dig the litter grains, like the queen would do, to get the kitten to come and start his elimination sequence.

- Often likes to eat litter grains, so I would prefer not using a clumping litter, unless the previous owner is certain the kitten never eats it.

If a kitten, or an adult cat, was living outside, and I want him to stay inside[4], I would:

---

[4] I would never try to keep inside a feral (wild) cat unless he is under 12 weeks of age. What I write is about domesticated cats that are used to pee and poo outside.

1) Keep house plants out of reach for at least a month or install a plastic over the soil of each plant.

2) Prefer pellet or permanent sand litter and use the technique of mixing with live turf or soil (see "Moving to Pellet Litter" and "Moving to Permanent Sand Litter").

Step-by-step:

1) It is not possible to do a preliminary habituation to a room before the kitten has to use his new litter. To avoid the risk of a bad association:

    a. I choose a quiet room that can be closed.

    b. I ask the earlier owner what type of litter the kitten used (size, brand, and variety, open or close). I buy the same thing and install it in the room.

2) I place the kitten in the room as soon as he arrives.

3) I carry out the confinement procedure.

4) I carry out the anchoring procedure.

5) If the house is very spacious or has two floors, I would install a second litter, so the kitten is never too far away from a litter.

Moving from One Room to Another

Picture 10) This is a "three-wall setup". I make sure it is solid and stable.

I disagree with the proposal many people have made to move the litter foot by foot from its original place to its destination room. First, it is often not possible for various reasons. More importantly, the cat needs to habituate to all intermediary places, which is unnecessarily difficult.

The original idea I present here is the use of a decoration or specific setup. With a setup that makes the move with the litter, the cat will see and smell, at least in part, the same surroundings as before the move. This way, when the cat goes in the litter in the new room, it feels like in his usual elimination place, giving him a sense of safety. This is exactly what the cat needs to start his elimination. Bottom line, when making a single move with a piece of décor, the cat only needs to habituate to one new setting and one new room.

Of course, using a piece of décor to move from one room to another is not always necessary. If the cat is using an enclosed litter box, it is his décor, so he doesn't need any décor added. A very self-confident cat, habituated to the new room, doesn't need a piece of décor either. On the other hand, I would certainly use it for an unsecure cat. I would also use it if I absolutely want to minimize the risk of any inappropriate elimination. For instance, if I have very expensive carpets I want to mitigate the risk of them getting ruined. Whenever I can't habituate the cat to the new room before moving the litter in, the décor will help. For instance, a piece of décor is extremely helpful if I must bring my cat on vacation or if I must move to a new house.

I propose using a setup made from cardboard because it is cheap, odor-absorbing, cuts a bit of the sound out, obscures the view (has opacity), and is widely available. Cardboard is also easy to cut and to manipulate. Any product with the same properties will do. I must never wash it because it would change its smell. When the change is complete, I dump it.

I carry out the regularity check and anchoring after every step.

Step-by-step:

1) If possible, I carry out the preliminary habituation to the new room.

2) Meanwhile, I create a setup close to the place the litter is presently.

a) If the litter is next to a wall, I stick a piece of cardboard about thirty-six by thirty-six inches (90 X 90 centimeters) on the wall.

b) If the litter is more than thirty-six inches (ninety centimeters) from any wall, I make a three-wall décor with cardboard and place it one foot from the litter. I make sure it is stable.

c) In the unlikely event that the cat starts to make inappropriate eliminations, it means the cat is uncomfortable with this new décor. I need to place it away from the litter and bring it progressively closer to the litter over seven days.

3) I take the décor and the litter and move them directly to the new room. I place the cardboard next to the litter in the same way as before the move.

a) If the litter was close to a wall, I place the litter close to a wall and install the cardboard on the wall.

b) If the litter was more than thirty-six inches (ninety centimeters) from a wall, I can either:

I) Place the litter more than thirty-six inches from a wall and install the three-walls décor as before, one foot from the litter.

II) Place the litter as close as one foot from a wall (but not any closer) and install the three-wall décor as before; one foot from the litter.

4) I remove the décor.

Moving to Pellet Litter

When I change a litter type, I do not change the location of the litter box. Also, everything close to the litter must stay as it used to be. This is a familiar "piece of décor" that contributes to triggering elimination. As always, I carry out regularity check and anchoring after every step.

Assuming my cat is not using clumping granular litter.

Step-by-step:

1) I discard the litter contents and clean the litter as usual. I fill the litter with the same amount of grain as usual minus one cup (250 ml). I add one cup of pellets to the litter box. I mix it with the contents of the litter.

2) I discard the contents of the litter and clean. I fill it with three-quarters litter grains and one-quarter pellets. I mix the content of the litter.

3) I discard the contents of the litter and clean. I fill it half with litter grains and half with pellets. I mix the content of the litter.

4) I discard the contents of the litter and clean. I fill it with one-quarter litter grains, and three-quarters pellets. I mix the contents of the litter.

5) I discard the contents of the litter and clean. I fill it with three to four inches (7.5 to 10 centimeters) of pellets only.

6) We live happily ever after.

Assuming my cat is using a clumping, granular litter and I want to move to pellets: At first the litter will still clump. So, instead of removing only poo, I will be able to remove pee too; that's great. After a certain quantity of pellets are added, the litter will stop clumping. So, I would need to go on with the procedure as above. That means I will dump clumping litter even if it has only been in use for one week and even if it is guaranteed to be good for forty days. I am convinced this is necessary.

Otherwise, the litter would get full of pee spread all over and the cat would avoid the litter.

If my cat used to go out on the lawn for his pee and poo and I want to get him to eliminate in the house, green pellets are a good choice. In this case, I would need to use confinement after each change. The cat will definitely be withholding his pee and poo, and confinement will probably need to last forty-eight hours rather than the usual twenty-four hours. The ideal situation is to start with a litter that has live turf on the bottom and start adding pellets over it. The second best option is to use earth taken from the area where the cat used to go and start adding pellets and mixing. If I don't have access to outside earth, I would use potting soil.

Moving to Permanent Sand Litter

I do no change at all with respect to the location of the litter box. Also, everything close to the litter must stay as it used to be. This is the familiar “décor” which contributes to triggering elimination. I will place the old litter somewhere the cat can’t access, nor view nor smell. As before, I carry out regularity check and anchoring after every step.

Assuming my cat is using a non-clumping granular litter and I want to move to permanent sand.

Step-by-step:

1) I discard the litter content and clean the litter box. I add one inch of sand and three inches of the old granular product. I mix the contents of the litter.

2) I discard the litter contents and clean the litter box. I add two inches of sand and two inches of the old granular product. I mix the contents of the litter.

3) I discard the litter contents and clean the litter box. I add three inches of sand and one inch of the old granular product. I mix the contents of the litter.

4) I discard the litter contents and clean the litter box. I add four inches of sand only.

5) I discard the old litter box. I prepare the doubled litter box as described above, adding four inches of sand.

6) And we've been dreaming of sandy beaches ever after.

Assuming my cat is using a clumping granular litter and I want to move to permanent sand: At first the litter will still clump so instead of removing only poo, I will be able to remove pee too. That's great. After a certain quantity of sand is added, the litter will stop clumping. So, I need to go on with the procedure as stated above. That means I will dump some clumping litter even if it has been in use just one week and even if it is guaranteed to be good for forty days. I am convinced this is necessary otherwise the litter would get full of pee spread all over and the cat would avoid the litter for that very reason.

If my cat used to go out over soil for his pee and poo and I want to get him to eliminate in the house, permanent sand is a good choice. In this case, I would need to use confinement after each change. The cat will definitely be withholding his pee and poo, and confinement will probably need to last forty-eight hours rather than the usual twenty-four hours. I would start with a litter having soil taken in the area where the cat is used to going and start adding sand as described above.

Moving into a Bath or Shower

I have already explained how I move the litter from one room to another. So, let's assume the litter is in the bathroom and I want to move it into a shower with no wall to jump over or to block the view (called a "walk-in" shower):

1) I call the cat into the shower and when he comes, I give him a treat. I repeat it nine times a day for a week. If the cat doesn't come when I call him, I can leave two or three treats in the shower. I make sure the cat sees them. When the cat has eaten them, I put others in, making sure the cat went in there nine times every day. Alternatively, I can leave his bowl of food and water in the shower. If the shower is often used, it is important to practice until the cat doesn't mind walking over some water residue.

2) I move the litter exactly where I want it in the shower.

3) I clean the floor where the litter was.

If the cat needs to jump over a wall, such as jumping over the side of a bath, he needs an extra step. In the bottom of the bath, the environment is different. Using a cardboard setup in a wet place is not practical. At first, the cat needs to be able to see the bathroom while he eliminates. More specifically, when the cat stands in his litter, his eyes should be over the level of the side of the bath. This is true for the first week only. So, I would go ahead as above, habituating the cat to the bath, except that when I move the litter into the bath, I would place it on a stand just high enough. I would make sure the stand is very stable. Then, I would remove the stand in one single step.

Moving to Water Litter

I buy a set of three bowls that will fit in the water litter box with the cover closed. All bowls should be identical except for their size. One bowl should be about four inches (10 centimeters) in diameter, the other should be about seven inches (18 centimeters) in diameter and the other about ten inches (25 centimeters) in diameter.

I place the water litter, with the bowls inside (but without water in the bowls), and the cover closed, next to the granular litter, so the cat can habituate to those objects.

Meanwhile, I acclimate the cat to the sounds and sights that occur when liquid and solid fall into water. Every day for seven days, I take the large bowl, fill it with three inches (7.5 centimeters) of water and place it in the water litter. I then take a cup of water, place it three inches (7.5 centimeters) above the litter and slowly poor the water from the cup to the bowl. I then take a three inches (7.5 centimeter) long piece of carrot or celery, place it three inches (7.5 centimeters) above the litter and drop it in the water. I do this while the cat is close by and give him a treat after each instance. I don’t let the cat play or “fish” in the water. I repeat this nine times. Afterward, I remove the water from the bowl. I don’t want the cat to drink in that bowl. Otherwise, he will not want to use it for pee or poo later.

I carry out regularity check and anchoring after every step. If in a room that can be closed, I can carry out confinement and anchoring after every step for more safety. Note that when the bowl is moved slowly over seven days the anchoring is occurring as the bowl moves and I confine the cat only the first day each time a new bowl is introduced.

Step-by-step:

1) I remove the cover and pour the contents of the granular litter into the water litter box.

2) I place the cover back on the water box.

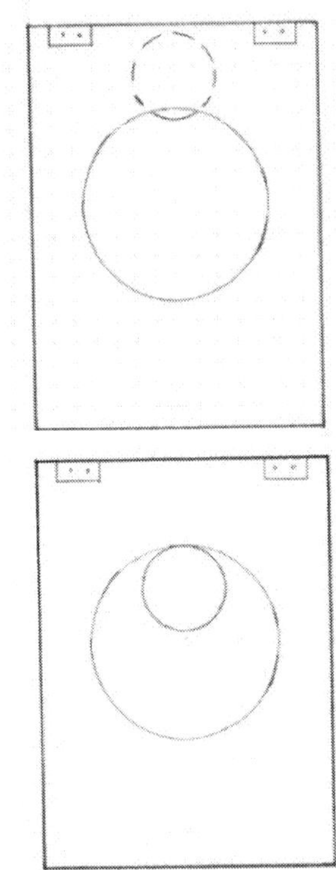

Picture 11: This is how I would move the small bowl of water from the first day to the seventh day.

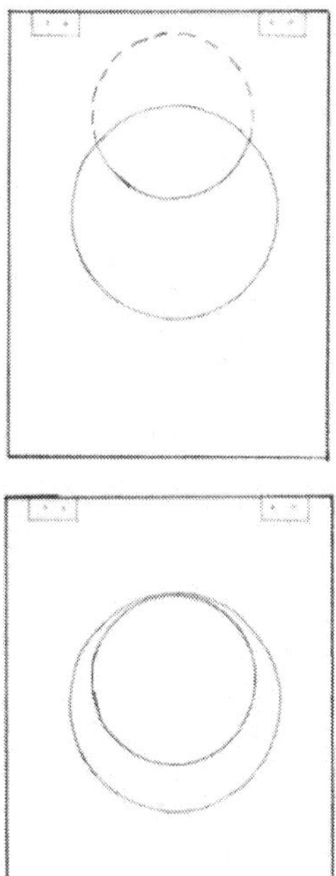

Picture 12: This is how I would move the medium bowl of water from the first day to the seventh day.

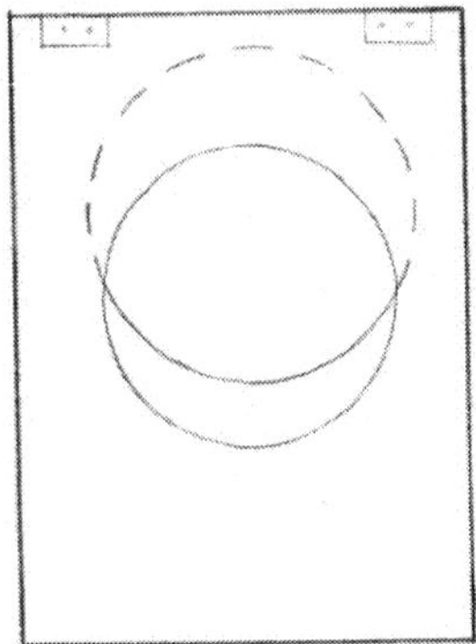

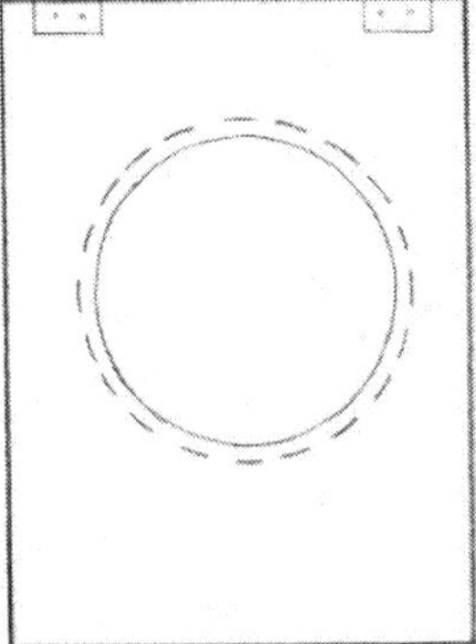

Picture 13: This is how I would move the large bowl of water from the first day to the seventh day.

3) I install the small bowl, with three inches (7.5 centimeters) of water in it, close to the back of the litter. Over the next seven days I will slowly move it from the back toward the center of the hole. I stop when the back of the bowl is just flush with the seat opening.

4) I remove the small bowl and install the medium bowl, with three inches (7.5 centimeters) of water in it, close to the back of the litter. Over the next seven days I will slowly move it from the back toward the center of the hole. I stop when the back of the bowl is just flush with the seat opening.

5) I remove the medium bowl and install the large bowl, with three inches (7.5 centimeters) of water in it, close to the back of the litter. Over the next seven days, I will slowly move it from the back to the center of the hole.

Note: During the three previous steps, the cat will scrape the grains of litter and will often pour some into the bowl. I would dump it and replace the water. I would also dump any pee or poo that would end up in the bowl.

6) Now that the large bowl is in the center of the litter, litter grains are not accessible to the cat. However, I leave litter grains around the bowl, inside the box, during the anchoring. The smell of those litter grains at that place are telling the cat to keep doing his pee and poo there.

7) I dump the grains and clean the water box. I put the bowl back in place with three inches (7.5 centimeters) of water.

8) And we lived "grain free" ever after.

Moving to the Toilet

I make sure the cat can't drink in the toilet bowl, so I keep the toilet cover closed until the cat starts using the toilet for pees and poos. Also, I make sure the cat won't be able to drop anything in the toilet bowl. Example: I don't leave anything on the toilet tank.

I previously wrote that my method will progressively guide the cat so that he ends up placing himself properly on the toilet seat. That means the back of the cat is toward the water tank of the toilet, his face looking away, just like us when sitting on a toilet. I have developed two tricks to achieve that.

The setup:

The water litter is a rectangular box. Let's call its longer dimension the length. The water litter will be placed at about six inches (15 centimeters) from a wall, with its <u>length perpendicular to that wall</u>. On that wall, I will place a piece of cardboard about thirty-six X thirty-six inches (90 X 90 centimeters); let's call it the back cardboard. On the water litter a toilet seat will be installed with the two screws of the seat at about six inches (15 centimeters) from the wall with the back cardboard. Later, when the cat moves to the real toilet, the back cardboard will cover the front of the water tank. Proceeding like that ensures that the orientation of the toilet seat with respect to the back carboard doesn't change. As a result, the cat doesn't get disoriented.

The progression of the water bowl in the water litter:

In the section "Moving to Water Litter," I wrote that I move the water bowls from the back of the litter toward the center. Let's define the back of the litter as the side of the litter that is closest to the wall with the back cardboard. As I introduce the water bowls at the back and make them progress toward the front, the cat moves his legs away from the water bowl. If the sizes of the bowls are chosen as indicated, and the progression is done as suggested, the cat will end up perfectly placed on the seat.

Where would I place the litter before the move?

That depends on the limitations of my bathroom, but here are some examples:

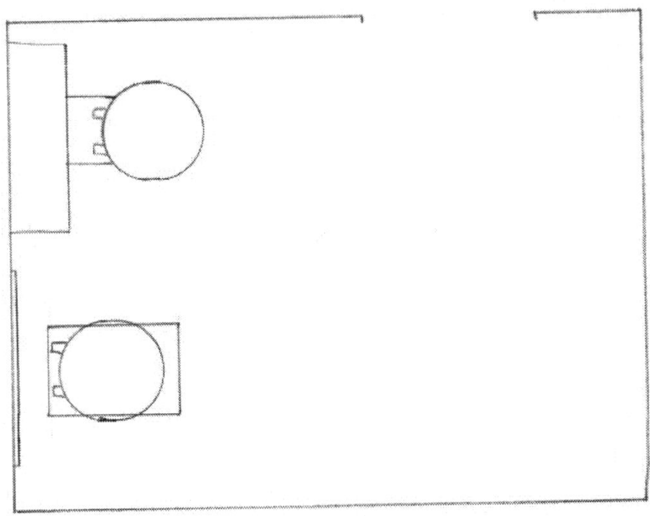

Picture 14: Ideal: Side by side, same orientation as the toilet, close to the toilet.

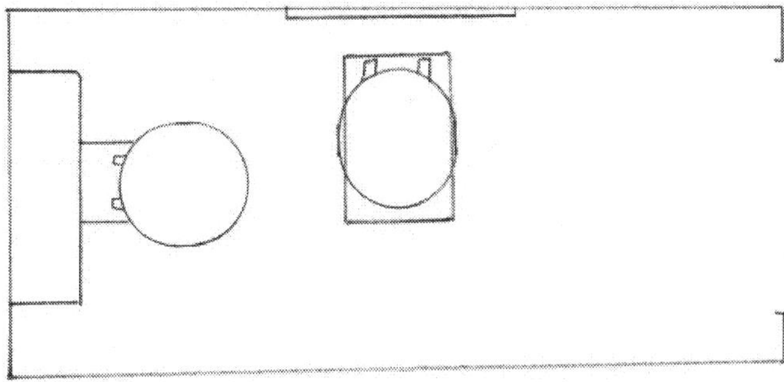

Picture 15: Good: 90 degrees from the toilet's orientation, close to the toilet.

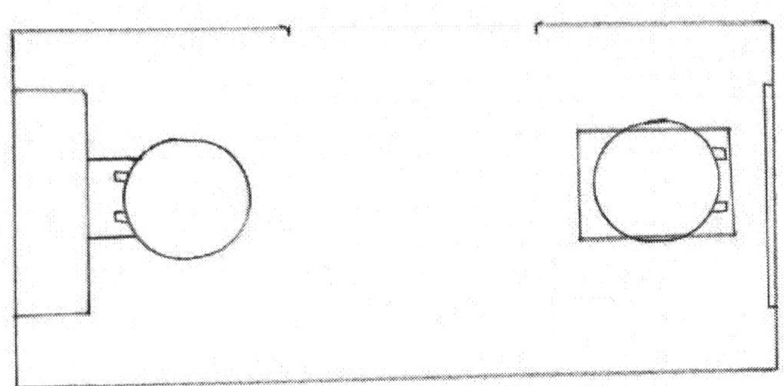

Picture 16: Acceptable: 180 degrees from the toilet's orientation, far from the toilet.

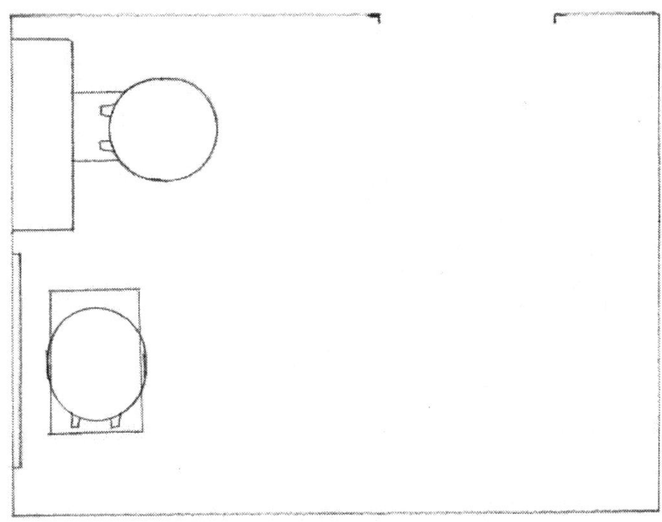

Picture 17: Bad: Litter length not perpendicular to the wall with the back cardboard.

At first, those requirements may seem unnecessary. But, please remember that elimination is a behavioral sequence. The cat is on autopilot, or like a sleepwalker. I don't want the cat to have to ask himself questions like "well, let's see, how should I proceed here, how am I going to place myself?" I want the cat's state of mind to be "Business as usual, let's just do it." Giving the cat a décor and an orientation as guideline is a key of success here.

Toilet seat

At some point during the training, I will need a toilet seat for the cat on his water litter, and another on my toilet. The toilet seat that the cat will use for his training is the one that will move to my toilet at the end of the training. That is the seat that the humans and the cat will end up sharing.

I want this seat to be stable when fixed to my toilet bowl, so the attachments at the back of the seat must match perfectly with their intended holes at the back of the toilet bowl.

I want this seat to be solid. Solid wood is great; either painted or varnished. Some cheap plastic seats tend to bend or slide horizontally, so I would not use them. In one book, it is suggested to use a padded seat to help the cat stand on the seat. Healthy cats don't need padding to stand on the seat. I think they might use their claws to try to bury their pee and poo and destroy the padding. If the cat is declawed or handicapped and seems to have difficulty not sliding, I would install a platform next to the seat. A platform is also great for cats who are severely overweight, very old, or that have joint pain.

Leaky Toilet Technique

Even though all cats can learn to activate the toilet flush, I would not teach them that. The sucking power that flushing produces is strong enough to hurt or even kill a full-grown cat. The possibility that the cat falls in the toilet after activating the flush would haunt me. Also, the first sign of several health issues is visible in the poos: diarrhea, constipation, blood as well as other irregularities, and I would not want to miss it. What I find very convenient is to, instead, leave a constant fine water flow when I am not there to flush regularly. There are no guarantees that it will get rid of all the poos, but it will ensure no bad smell can develop.

There is a hole inside the water tank, by which the water goes from tank to bowl when I flush. After a flush completes, there is a cap that comes down over the hole and stops the water flow. I place a small stick between the cap and the hole, thus preventing the cap from completely closing the hole. Just a very small flow suffices.

I would not do it with a toilet that has a history of blockage, nor if I were living on the upper floor of an apartment building. However, I would do it in my basement toilet. Please use your best judgement: I expressly deny any liability for loss, damage or injury caused, directly or indirectly, if you choose to use that technique.

Stepping Up

Everywhere I looked, people recommended raising the litter box progressively until it is at the same height than the toilet seat. Some books suggest simply placing a pile of newspapers or books under the litter to lift it. This was indeed part of the technique I learned in the eighties. What happens is that each time the cat jumps in or out, the litter slides a bit. It has become clear to me that the litter doesn't need to fall off the pile; a very small slip is already a serious problem.

Proceeding like that needed the cat to learn either:

1) To jump in and out of an unstable object without making it react: a pretty difficult task physically.

2) Or, to ignore a basic instinct that exists to ensure its safety. Making an animal go against his instinct is one of the most difficult and lengthy processes.

Moreover, those lessons have nothing to do with my goal of toilet training.

From a cat's point of view, moving a litter by ten inches (25 centimeters) upward, is not stranger than moving a litter by ten inches (25 centimeters) horizontally. Of course, this is only true if the upper installation is perfectly stable.

Just like when I move a litter from one room to another with its décor and save pointless intermediate learning steps, I now go in one single strep from a toilet seat at six inches (15 centimeters) to sixteen inches (41 centimeters) from the ground and directly over my toilet bowl.

Odor Transfer

Because odor is so important for cats, it should be obvious that the main key is to habituate them to use a litter that smells like the human toilet. Unfortunately, this is mentioned nowhere. The week before the move to the toilet, I rub toilet paper on the horizontal surface on top of the toilet bowl. Then, I use that toilet paper to rub the cat's water bowl, just above the water level. The first time I do just a little rubbing, the next day a bit more, and so on for seven days. I will clean the toilet before the move to make the smell more acceptable, but the cat will also have other things to get used to: the shape of the bowl, the level of water, and perhaps other changes I can't perceive. I try to make one single change at once, so this step is more than required.

I assume the litter is already in the toilet room. As usual, I carry out confinement and anchoring after each step.

Step-by-step:

Picture 18: The back cardboard on the wall and the litter inside the cardboard box.

1) I place the litter as described above:

    a. With regard to the wall on which I install a back cardboard.

    b. With regard to the toilet.

2) I make a box of cardboard just big enough to enclose the litter. I fold the bottom flaps inward. I fold the top flaps downward inside. I place the litter inside the cardboard box.

3) I start the "odor transfer" as described above.

Picture 19: The back cardboard fixed over the front of the toilet tank. The three sides of the cardboard box (front, left and right) fixed around the toilet tank. The bottom flaps down. The top flaps folded toward the inside. A bumper (cork cap) is installed. The toilet is readily usable by human without anything to put on and off.

4) Move to the toilet:

a. I fix the back carboard over the front of the toilet tank (I cut an opening to be able to flush).

b. I fix three sides of the cardboard box (front, left and right) around the toilet tank, letting the bottom flaps down and folding downward inside the top flaps.

c. I install the water litter seat on my toilet; I fix the screws and make sure it is solid and stable.

d. If the level of water in the toilet bowl is much lower than what the cat is used to I <u>slowly</u> add some water to raise the level (if possible). I do that the first week, then I progressively let the cat acclimate to a lower water level.

e. I don't use a seat cover: That way, nobody can inadvertently close the cover.

f. Installing a bumper over the back carboard ensures the seat can't stay up without someone holding it. The seat can never be mistakenly left upward.

g. I wash the floor of the whole bathroom.

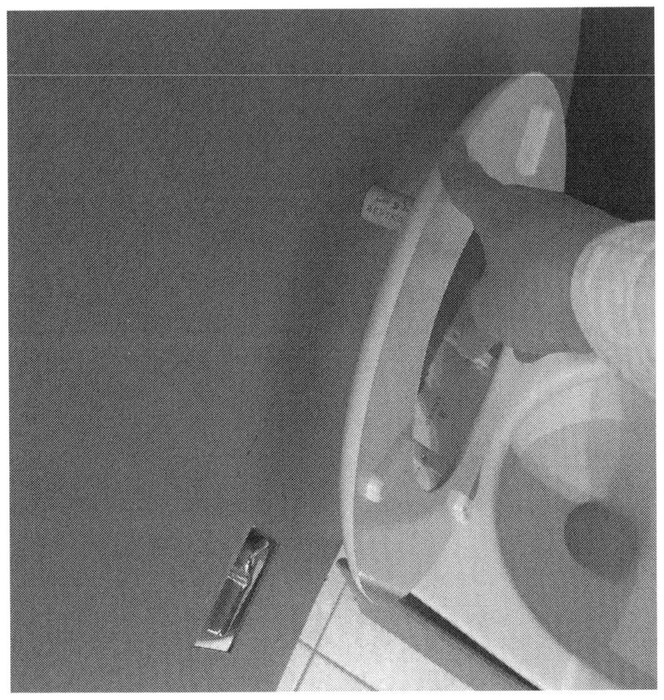

Picture 20: A bumper over the back carboard ensures the seat can't stay up without someone holding it. The seat can never be mistakenly left upward.

5) Over the following weeks, I progressively get rid of the setup; piece by piece: the left part, right part, and front part of cardboard box. Then I reduce the size of

the back cardboard until nothing is left. The cat doesn’t need confinement for this step.

6) And we lived litter free ever after.

PART VI

Test Your Knowledge

Assuming you are going to have a baby (or a dog) and you don't want him to bother the cat when he's sleeping: You don't want the baby to have access to the cat litter. Your toilet is already too crowded, so you don't want to train the cat to use the toilet. You also want to save space. What could you do?

They are many possible solutions, find yours, then go to next page to see what I would do.

?

Picture 21: Cat's structure outside and inside.

An old bookcase was used to build this structure. The structure needs to be screwed to the wall to be solid and stable when the cat jumps on it. It is perfect for a cat that has all his claws and who's not overweight. If the cat has difficulties climbing, a chair can be placed close by. At about three feet (ninety centimeters) from the ground, I modified a shelf to make it more like a fixed drawer. In the “drawer,” I installed the litter box. It could also be water litter. There is some space on the bottom to place books and/or the cat’s things close by.

The cat can access its litter climbing from the ground (or from a chair) through a hole on the side. He can also access it through a hole on the top of the structure. Most cats love to relax in high places and look around. The cat can relax in peace when he sleeps on the top, or he can use his litter without getting disturbed. He will like scratching with his claws on the sides, telling everybody that it is his reserved area.

Because the litter is not at the same level as the sleeping place, and because there is a curtain to obscure the view and the odor coming from the litter, this relative proximity of the litter and sleeping area should be accepted by most cats.

Now, assume the cat’s litter is currently in another room on the floor. What would you do to get the cat to adopt his new litter place? They are many possible solutions, find yours, then go to the next page to see what I would do.

?

I would install a three wall setup around the litter and progressively bring it closer until it is flush with three sides of the litter.

1) In the meantime, I would acclimate the cat to his new place and make sure he likes it. I would check that he can jump in and out without difficulty. If not, I would install a chair close by.

2) I would move the litter with the piece of décor inside the structure in one single step.

3) Over the following weeks, I would progressively get rid of the décor, piece by piece.

Empowerment

"Give a man a fish and you feed him for a day; teach a man to fish and you feed him for a lifetime."- Anne Isabella Thackeray Ritchie

Over the years, publicity and public culture have shaped cat owners' behavior (ha, ha, ha!). Most are now convinced that buying litter grain over and over is a necessity.

I gave you the information to understand cats' elimination behavior and some of their learning process. To inspire you, I also gave you a few specific examples of how I would make the changes. Now, you have all the pieces. They are yours to mix and match to fit each specific need you and your cat have. I suggest that you make a written list of all the steps that you will need and figure out exactly how you will achieve each before you start. This way you avoid ending up at a dead end. It also allows you to optimize your procedure to make it as easy as possible for your cat.

The knowledge you have now makes you free and capable of making your own litter choices. That's why I call this collection Pet Owners' Freedom.

Epilogue

If you do some research, you will realize there are a lot of people out there who don't know how to go ahead with litter changes. On one side, they are pseudo experts that write all sorts of nonsense and use gadgets that only complicate the process. On the other side, they are pet owners looking for advice. Although it is perfectly legitimate to want to save money or to be tired of cleaning, I worry that people are ready to try any trick at the risk of making their cat crazy. As mentioned earlier, when the cat gets unclean, he is at risk of abandonment.

Do you believe the method and tools I present in this book will help both owners and cats to succeed with their litter changes? Do you believe this book can contribute to reducing uncleanliness and abandonment? Have you successfully realized some changes inspired by my method?

I am counting on the value of my method and the quality of information contained in this book to convince you to talk with your friends and on social media about this book.

If you like the book, a powerful way to help is to leave a review on Amazon.

If you have a web site or blog, you are more than welcome to place a link toward my book and eBook web page on Amazon.

On the other hand, for comments and suggestions to improve the book, please email me at LitterFreeFreedom@yahoo.com I will gladly take your insightful comments into account in the next edition.

Hopping you will help me contribute to cats' wellbeing, I wish you a long and happy life with your loved one(s).

Thanks a lot,

Claude Bois

Please do not remove these encrypted strings proving my copyright ownership:

SHA 256:

420c90b43a6375a84c2ca507bcbecca87e0f6fc7a2d7afd

3d10487768dc56199

BCRYPT:

$2y$10$qibYuNDdhVvpoyGDBieNvuzVQPRAZ8sMwBJzB

POXojTQt.WQiooku

41803776R00091

Made in the USA
Middletown, DE
13 April 2019